ESCAPE, RESCUE, & SURVIVAL

MOUNTAINS AND WILDERNESS
Amazing Real-Life Stories!

CHRIS SCHWAB

ROURKE'S SCHOOL to HOME CONNECTIONS
BEFORE AND DURING READING ACTIVITIES

Before Reading: *Building Background Knowledge and Vocabulary*

Building background knowledge can help children process new information and build upon what they already know. Before reading a book, it is important to tap into what children already know about the topic. This will help them develop their vocabulary and increase their reading comprehension.

Questions and Activities to Build Background Knowledge:

1. Look at the front cover of the book and read the title. What do you think this book will be about?
2. What do you already know about this topic?
3. Take a book walk and skim the pages. Look at the table of contents, photographs, captions, and bold words. Did these text features give you any information or predictions about what you will read in this book?

Vocabulary: *Vocabulary Is Key to Reading Comprehension*

Use the following directions to prompt a conversation about each word.
- Read the vocabulary words.
- What comes to mind when you see each word?
- What do you think each word means?

Vocabulary Words:
- distress signal
- tourniquet
- Indigenous
- venom
- ominous
- wilderness

During Reading: *Reading for Meaning and Understanding*

To achieve deep comprehension of a book, children are encouraged to use close reading strategies. During reading, it is important to have children stop and make connections. These connections result in deeper analysis and understanding of a book.

 ### Close Reading a Text

During reading, have children stop and talk about the following:
- Any confusing parts
- Any unknown words
- Text to text, text to self, text to world connections
- The main idea in each chapter or heading

Encourage children to use context clues to determine the meaning of any unknown words. These strategies will help children learn to analyze the text more thoroughly as they read.

When you are finished reading this book, turn to the next-to-last page for **After-Reading Questions** and an **Activity**.

Table of Contents

When Animals Attack

A Black Bear Scare 5
A Harrowing Hike 10

Lost!

Alone in the Amazon 14
Desert Distress 18

Injured and Alone

Plane Crash in Peru 22
Canyon Catastrophe 26

Memory Game 30
Index 31
After-Reading Questions 31
Activity 31
About the Author 32

Mountains and wilderness areas are the perfect places to have fun outdoors. But in these wide-open spaces, danger can be right around the corner!

When Animals Attack

A Black Bear Scare

One night in 2017, as camp counselor Dylan McWilliams slept under the Colorado stars in his sleeping bag, he awoke to an awful noise—

CRUNCH!

When Animals Attack

Dylan's head was inside the mouth of a black bear, and its teeth were crunching down on his skull.

He was in trouble! As the bear dragged him toward the woods, Dylan screamed, punched the bear, and poked it in the eyes.

BLACK BEARS' TEETH CAN MEASURE TWO-AND-A-HALF INCHES (6.4 CENTIMETERS) LONG!

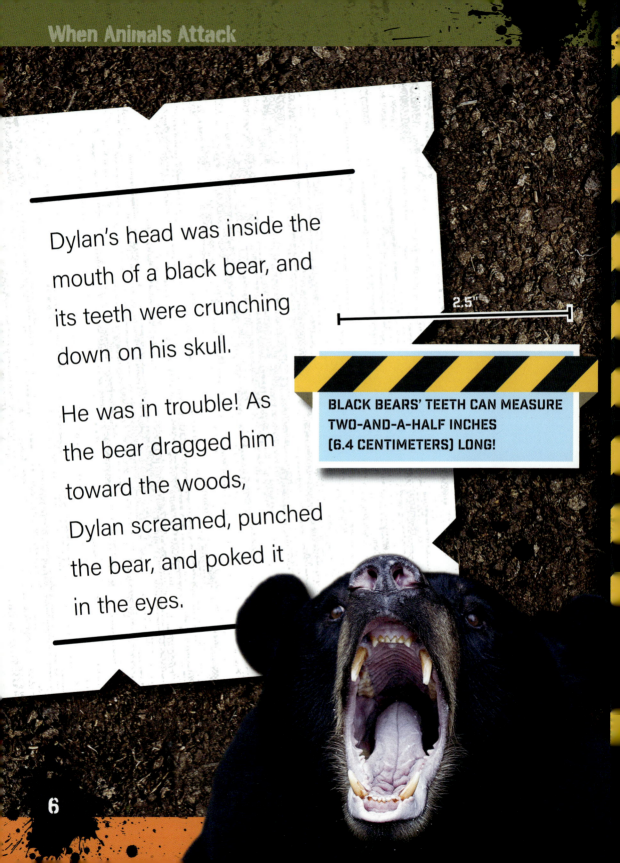

When Animals Attack

Mauled by a Sloth Bear

Who: teenager Pinky Baiga
Where: central India
What: attacked by a sloth bear, one of the country's deadliest animals
Details: spent ten days in the hospital

Startled awake by all the noise, other counselors ran to help. They scared the bear, and it lumbered off into the woods. Dylan was taken by ambulance to the hospital where doctors stapled his head wounds closed.

This story could've had quite a different ending if Dylan hadn't fought back. Because of his strength and quick thinking, he survived.

SURVIVING A BEAR ATTACK

- DON'T RUN—YOU CAN'T OUTRUN A BEAR.
- DON'T CLIMB A TREE—BEARS CAN CLIMB BETTER.
- IF IT'S A BLACK BEAR, FIGHT BACK.
- IF IT'S A BROWN OR GRIZZLY BEAR, PLAY DEAD.

When Animals Attack

A Harrowing Hike

Bears aren't the only wild animals to watch out for in the woods. Just ask Scott Vuncannon.

In 2018, equipped with bear spray and enough food and water for a couple days, he and his dog, Boone, went on a day hike in North Carolina's Nantahala National Forest. He told his wife they'd be home midafternoon.

When Animals Attack

Five miles into the hike, Scott heard it— the **ominous** rattle. But the warning was too late. He had already been struck in the leg.

IF A VENOMOUS SNAKE BITES

DO:
- MOVE OUT OF ITS STRIKING RANGE
- LIE OR SIT WITH THE BITE BELOW THE LEVEL OF YOUR HEART
- CALL 911
- GET MEDICAL HELP IMMEDIATELY

DON'T:
- APPLY A TOURNIQUET
- SLICE OPEN THE WOUND OR SUCK OUT THE VENOM
- ICE OR SOAK THE WOUND
- DRINK CAFFEINE

ominous (AH-muh-nuhs): signaling trouble ahead

tourniquet (TUR-nuh-kit): a device that stops bleeding

venom (VEN-uhm): poison made by certain snakes, insects, and other animals

When Animals Attack

Scott yanked up his pant leg and saw two fang marks from a rattlesnake! He could taste the venom in his mouth. It was moving fast through his body. He checked his phone. No service!

Within minutes, Scott's vision got blurry. He began to sweat and throw up. He needed to get out of the mountains! But he quickly became unable to walk. Desperate and alone, he tried to crawl. He soon fell unconscious. Boone licked and pawed at him anxiously, staying right by his side.

When Animals Attack

Worried that her husband wasn't home by late afternoon and wasn't answering her texts, Scott's wife alerted a fire and rescue team. Something was wrong! They set out to look for him.

Deep within the woods, they found Scott near death with Boone curled up by his side. They carried him out of the woods, and he was flown by helicopter to the nearest hospital. He survived and is hiking again—all because he told his wife where he was going and when he would be home!

Lost!

Alone
in the Amazon

When Yossi Ghinsberg dreamed of jungle exploration, it didn't include being lost and alone in a rain forest with hungry animals and venomous snakes. But that's exactly what happened.

Lost in Lion Territory

Who: 12-year-old Alex Mboweni
Where: South African bush
What: separated from family when crossing border
Details: charged at by an elephant; dehydrated and starving; mother found him after eight days

Yossi, an Israeli citizen, was rafting with a friend through Bolivia's Amazon **wilderness** when the unimaginable happened. Their raft flipped! Yossi's friend made it to safety, but Yossi went tumbling over a waterfall. When he washed ashore down the river, he quickly realized he was alone.

wilderness (WIL-dur-nis): area of land where no people live

Lost!

For three weeks, Yossi wandered through the thick jungle. All he had was a backpack with a few camping supplies and a little bit of food. He ate anything he could find, including berries and chicken eggs.

Dangers surrounded him. Leeches sucked his blood. Termites covered his body. He sank to his chest in quicksand. He even stared down a jaguar but scared it away by lighting his can of bug spray on fire.

Lost!

Yossi was desperate. Using driftwood and a bright red poncho, he made a sign by the river. He had lost 35 pounds in three weeks and didn't have the strength to keep going. Then he heard it—a boat! His friend from the raft had found him with the help of an **Indigenous** tribe. He was rescued!

GRAB SOME POPCORN

YOSSI'S STORY WAS MADE INTO A MOVIE CALLED *JUNGLE*. DANIEL RADCLIFFE PLAYED YOSSI!

Indigenous (in-DIJ-uh-nuhs): of or relating to the earliest known inhabitants of a region

Lost!

Desert Distress

Seventy-two-year-old Ann Rodgers and her dog, Queenie, were driving through Arizona when her car came to a slow stop on a deserted road. She was out of gas! Surrounded by nothing but wilderness, they got out and hiked nearby hills hoping to get cell phone service. But no luck.

For the first few days, Ann and Queenie stayed in her car for warmth at night. But when they ran out of water, they headed toward a pond she had seen from a hilltop.

Over the next few days, they lived in a shelter Ann made. She drank clean water from a creek nearby and ate desert plants and berries she knew were safe. She even kept hot embers wrapped in moss so she would always be able to start a fire.

Lost!

Growing weaker and more worried, Ann gathered rocks and elk skeleton bones. She used them to write "HELP" in big letters on the ground. She tucked a note under a rock saying they were headed into the canyon. What a smart move!

After nine days of being lost, Ann and Queenie were finally rescued by searchers who saw her sign from a helicopter.

HUG-A-TREE AND SURVIVE

RULE NUMBER ONE IF YOU ARE LOST: STAY PUT! HUG A TREE. DON'T MOVE UNTIL YOU ARE FOUND.

Lost!

The group that rescued Ann said her **distress signal** led them to her.

She was weak and dehydrated, but she survived!

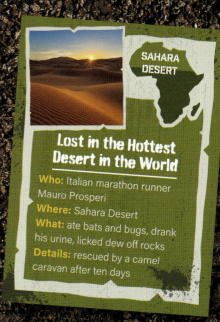

Lost in the Hottest Desert in the World

Who: Italian marathon runner Mauro Prosperi
Where: Sahara Desert
What: ate bats and bugs, drank his urine, licked dew off rocks
Details: rescued by a camel caravan after ten days

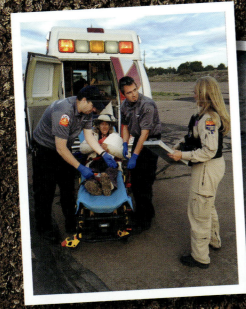

distress signal (di-STRESS SIG-nuhl): a message that one is in danger

Injured and Alone

Plane Crash in Peru

As the only survivor of a plane crash over a Peruvian rain forest, Juliane Koepcke knows what it is like to be injured and alone. After lightning struck her airplane, she was thrown out while still strapped to her seat. Juliane free-fell for two miles before landing in treetops.

Injured and Alone

Juliane suffered deep cuts, a concussion, and a broken collarbone. At just 17 years old, Juliane was stranded in a jungle with dangerous snakes, eight-foot caimans, and venomous spiders.

Injured and Alone

Juliane needed help. Her dad had always told her, "Follow the water if you are lost." So, that's what she did. She walked and swam for days. And then, she saw it—the crash site! She feasted on a bag of candy she found there.

Juliane continued to wander day and night until she came upon a hut. There, she pulled maggots out of the cuts on her arm. She was in pain, tired, and hungry. She had been lost for ten days.

Injured and Alone

The next day, Juliane was startled out of sleep by men's voices. She had been found by local fishermen! They took her out of the jungle and back to civilization by canoe. Juliane had survived not only a plane crash but a dangerous jungle too.

> "I ENDED UP EATING EVERYTHING THAT WOULD LET ME CATCH IT: TWO CRICKETS, FIVE OR SIX MOTHS, EIGHT OR TEN LARGE ANTS, AND THREE OR FOUR WATER BUGS."
>
> – GREG HEIN, LOST FOR SEVEN DAYS WITH A BROKEN LEG IN CALIFORNIA'S KINGS CANYON NATIONAL PARK

Injured and Alone

Canyon Catastrophe

Aron Ralston is an avid hiker and rock climber. But in 2003, his survival skills were put to the test when he set out to explore Utah's Bluejohn Canyon.

As Aron dropped into a narrow slot canyon to explore, the unimaginable happened—an 800-pound (363-kilogram) boulder fell and trapped his right hand against the canyon wall. His hand was crushed, and he was stuck! The pain was unbearable.

Injured and Alone

Aron was alone. No one knew where he was. He had no locator device. He carried only a few snacks, some water, and a small tool for digging, cutting, and slicing.

IT'S MOVIE NIGHT!

ARON'S UNBELIEVABLE STORY WAS MADE INTO THE MOVIE *127 HOURS*.

Injured and Alone

For days, Aron worked unsuccessfully to free himself. By the sixth day, he was out of water. He drank his own urine to stay hydrated. To survive, Aron knew he had no choice—he had to tie a tourniquet around his arm and cut off his hand.

Injured and Alone

Bleeding and in immense pain, Aron climbed out of the canyon. After hiking six miles back toward his truck, he came upon a family. They fed him, gave him water, and called rescuers. Aron survived to hike again another day. But now, he always tells someone where he's going.

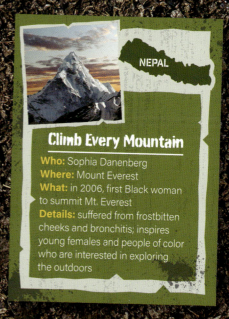

Climb Every Mountain

Who: Sophia Danenberg
Where: Mount Everest
What: in 2006, first Black woman to summit Mt. Everest
Details: suffered from frostbitten cheeks and bronchitis; inspires young females and people of color who are interested in exploring the outdoors

Memory Game

Look at the pictures. Can you retell what is happening in each image?

Index

canyon 20, 25, 26, 29

dehydrated 14, 21

desert 18, 19, 21

hiking 13, 29

jungle 14, 16, 17, 23, 25

mountain(s) 12, 29

rain forest 14, 22

rescued 17, 20, 21

1. Explain how to survive a bear attack.
2. What is "Rule Number One" if you are lost and alone?
3. What did Scott Vuncannon do that most likely saved his life?
4. What did Yossi and Ann both do that helped people find them?
5. Why does Aron now tell people where he is going hiking?

Activity

Most of these survivors carried or found at least one thing that helped them survive. Think about what you would want with you in the wild if you were attacked, lost, or injured. List at least ten things you would put in a survival kit for an adventure. Draw a picture of each item.

About the Author

Chris Schwab is a former teacher and writer currently living in Greensboro, North Carolina. She has hiked many mountains and deserts and encountered bears, snakes, javelinas, scorpions, and the random Gila monster—all without serious incident. She loves reading about other adventurers, the outdoors, and wildlife.

© 2024 Rourke Educational Media

All rights reserved. No part of this book may be reproduced or utilized in any form or by any means, electronic or mechanical including photocopying, recording, or by any information storage and retrieval system without permission in writing from the publisher.

www.rourkebooks.com

PHOTO CREDITS: Cover: ©zannadue/Shutterstock, ©Margaret.Wiktor/Shutterstock, ©Mike Treglia/Shutterstock, ©Joe McDonald/Shutterstock, ©Caprieleeeh/Shutterstock, ©Nadia Chi/Shutterstock, ©Tartila/Shutterstock; page 4: ©Ali Iyoob Photography/Shutterstock; page 5: ©Roschetzky Photography/Shutterstock; page 6: ©Jim Cumming/Shutterstock; page 7: ©Martin Mecnarowski/Shutterstock, ©Wyatt Rivard/Shutterstock; page 8: ©cleanfotos/Shutterstock; page 10: ©Chase D'animulls/Shutterstock; page 11: ©TempleNick/Shutterstock; page 12: ©Joe McDonald/Shutterstock; page 14: © Simon Dannhauer/Shutterstock; page 15: ©Noradoa/Shutterstock; page 16: ©Watch The World/Shutterstock, ©Travel Stock/Shutterstock; page 18: ©sstevens3/Shutterstock; page 19: ©Sheila Fitzgerald/Shutterstock; page 20: ©oneinchpunch/Shutterstock; page 21: ©Associated Press, ©Filipe B. Varela/Shutterstock; page 22: ©EL COMERCIO/El Comercio de PERU/Newscom; page 23: ©reptiles4all, ©Iafoto/Shutterstock; page 25: ©Mike Treglia; page 27: ©MICHAEL GERMANA / STAR MAX/Newscom; page 28: ©Galyna Andrushko/Shutterstock; page 29: ©Daniel Prudek/Shutterstock; page 30: ©Joe McDonald/Shutterstock, ©Noradoa/Shutterstock, ©sstevens3/Shutterstock, ©Iafoto/Shutterstock, ©Galyna Andrushko/Shutterstock, ©Daniel Prudek/Shutterstock

Edited by: Catherine Malaski
Cover design by: Nick Pearson
Interior design by: Nick Pearson

Library of Congress PCN Data

Mountains and Wilderness / Chris Schwab
(Escape, Rescue, and Survival)
ISBN 978-1-73165-735-0 (hard cover)
ISBN 978-1-73165-722-0 (soft cover)
ISBN 978-1-73165-748-0 (e-book)
ISBN 978-1-73165-761-9 (e-pub)
Library of Congress Control Number: 2023933220

Rourke Educational Media
Printed in the United States of America
01-1982311937